Nashua Public Library

Enjoy this book!
Please remember to return it on time
so that others may enjoy it too.

Manage your library account and
discover all we offer by visiting us
online at www.nashualibrary.org

Love your library? Tell a friend!

J

MERMAIDS

DO YOU BELIEVE?

This series features creatures that excite our minds. They're magical. They're mythical. They're mysterious. They're also not real. They live in our stories. They're brought to life by our imaginations. Facts about these creatures are based on folklore, legends, and beliefs. We have a rich history of believing in the impossible. But these creatures only live in fantasies and dreams. Monsters do not live under our beds. They live in our heads!

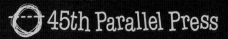

45th Parallel Press

Published in the United States of America by Cherry Lake Publishing
Ann Arbor, Michigan
www.cherrylakepublishing.com

Reading Adviser: Marla Conn MS, Ed., Literacy specialist, Read-Ability, Inc.
Book Design: Felicia Macheske

Photo Credits: © Willyam Bradberry,Shutterstock.com, cover, 7; © tsuneomp/Shutterstock.com, cover;
© Olga Nikonova/Shutterstock.com, 1; © schankz/Shutterstock.com, 1; © Alex Pix/Shutterstock.com, 5;
© Michael Bogner/Shutterstock.com, 8; © YorkBerlin/Shutterstock.com, 8; © Jaroslaw Grudzinski/
Shutterstock.com, 11; © Melkor3D/Shutterstock.com, 12; © Dmitry Laudin/Shutterstock.com, 15;
© Sergey Novikov/Shutterstock.com, 17;© S-F/Shutterstock.com, 18; © Dimitrina Lavchieva/Shutterstock.
com, 21; © Rudchenko Liliia/Shutterstock.com, 22; © prapann/Shutterstock.com, 24;
© MyColorfulPersonality/iStock, 27; © Detelina Petkova/Shutterstock.com, 29

Graphic Elements Throughout: © denniro/Shutterstock.com; © Libellule/Shutterstock.com; © sociologas/
Shutterstock.com; © paprika/Shutterstock.com; © ilolab/Shutterstock.com; © Bruce Rolff/Shutterstock.com

45th Parallel Press is an imprint of Cherry Lake Publishing.

Library of Congress Cataloging-in-Publication Data

Names: Loh-Hagan, Virginia, author.
Title: Mermaids / by Virginia Loh-Hagan.
Description: Ann Arbor : Cherry Lake Publishing, 2017. | Series: Magic, myth,
 and mystery | Includes bibliographical references and index.
Identifiers: LCCN 2016031787| ISBN 9781634721493 (hardcover) | ISBN
 9781634722810 (pbk.) | ISBN 9781634722155 (pdf) | ISBN 9781634723473 (ebook)
Subjects: LCSH: Mermaids—Juvenile literature.
Classification: LCC GR910 .L65 2017 | DDC 398.21—dc23
LC record available at https://lccn.loc.gov/2016031787

Cherry Lake Publishing would like to acknowledge the work of The Partnership for 21st Century Skills.
Please visit *www.p21.org* for more information.

Printed in the United States of America
Corporate Graphics

TABLE of CONTENTS

Chapter One

Under the Sea

How are mermaids different from Sirens? What do mermaids look like? What are the different types of mermaids?

"Beware the **Siren**!" Sailors are warned to be careful of Sirens. Sirens are monsters from Greek myths. They're half-women. They're half-birds. They sing beautiful songs. They distract sailors. They kill them.

Mermaids are magical sea creatures. They have a woman's body from their hips up. They have a fish tail. They live in oceans and seas. They live in rivers and lakes.

Mermaids are different from Sirens. But people confuse the two. It's because both creatures tempt sailors. They're known to bring sailors to their deaths. Siren is another word for a **vamp**. Vamps are women who charm men.

Mermaid *comes from an Old English word.*
Mere *means sea.* Maid *means a young woman.*

Explained by Science!

Water and air are different. Air has 20 times more oxygen than water. Water is heavier than air. Water is thicker than air. This means it takes more energy to breathe in water. Humans have lungs. They can't breathe underwater. Fish can. Fish use gills to breathe. Gills are like hundreds of tiny fingers on curved bars. Water passes through their gills. The gills remove the oxygen for the fish to use. Gills get rid of waste gases. Fish are cold-blooded. This means they need less oxygen. Humans are warm-blooded. Human lungs can't extract oxygen from water. Instead, water fills up lungs. This causes humans to drown.

Some mermaids have more dolphin-like tails.

Mermaids are beautiful. They're young. They carry a mirror. They like to look at themselves. They decorate their bodies. They use things they find in the water. They really like pretty shells.

They have long flowing hair. Their hair looks like sea foam. They carry a comb. They're often seen combing their hair on rocks.

Some have webbed hands. They have large, forked tails. Their tails are longer than legs. They're different colors. Their whole bodies **shimmer**. They shine.

Mermaids live together. Male mermaids are called **mermen**. There aren't many mermen. Together, they're **merfolk**.

Mermaids eat different things. Some eat seafood. Some eat only sea plants. Some eat humans.

There are different types of mermaids. They live all over the world. Most mermaids only live in the sea. They can't go on land.

Some mermaids shed their skins. They go to land. They get dry. Their tails become legs. They can walk on land. But they can only do this for a short time.

Some mermaids are **shapeshifters**. They can change into humans at any time. They can live in water and on land.

Mermaids adapt to the waters they live in.

More Than Swimming Beauties

What are mermaids' powers? How are they helpful? How are they not helpful?

Mermaids guide ships. They help lost ships find their way. But they also do bad things. They lead ships into rocks. They cause shipwrecks. They drown sailors. They drag them down. They squeeze out their lives. They collect their souls.

Mermaids have beautiful voices. They use their voices. They lure sailors. They enslave sailors. They get sailors to do things for them. They **hypnotize** sailors. This means they put them in a trance. Then, they control their actions. They erase their memories.

Mermaids have also saved sailors. They kiss sailors. This allows sailors to breathe underwater. Mermaids save them from drowning.

Full moons can grant mermaids extra or stronger powers.

Mermaids control the sea. They can bring life. They supply the sea with food. This means humans won't go hungry. But when mad, they can rid the sea of food. This means humans will go hungry.

They control weather. They cause storms. They cause calm seas. They control wind and air. They control water. They can move water. They can make water into different shapes. They can make balls of water. They can make ice. They can boil water. They can turn water to jelly.

They're excellent swimmers. Their tails allow them to swim really fast. They're excellent divers.

Some sailors thought mermaids were bad omens.

When Fantasy Meets Reality!

Explorers thought they saw merfolk. But they really saw sirenians. Sirenians are water animals. They're sometimes called sea cows. They include manatees and dugongs. They live in swamps, rivers, marine wetlands, and coastal marine waters. Sirenians have flat tails. Their tails are like paddles. They have flippers that look like stubby arms. Their flippers are used to steer. They look fat. But they're not. They're muscular. They have special skulls. They take breaths of air at the surface. They're herbivores. This means they eat sea plants. They constantly move to seek food. They don't leave the water. They make chirping sounds. They make barking sounds. Some stories say that sirenians used to be humans. These humans were cursed. They were changed into sirenians.

Mermaids have strong night vision. They can see in the total darkness of the deep sea.

Mermaids are smart. They use tools. They make weapons from things found in the sea. They make **tridents**. Tridents are like spears with three points. Their tridents are made of whale bone and shark teeth.

Mermaids can bring good fortune. They have healing powers. They grant wishes to humans. They can see the future.

Mermaids only have power when in water. They're connected to their water worlds. They talk to sea animals. They command sea animals.

They're strong. Their tails throw powerful kicks. Some are **immortal**. Immortal means they can live forever. They're **ageless**. They're always young.

Chapter Three

Managing Mermaids

What are mermaids' weaknesses?

Mermaids lose power on land. They get confused. They're out of their element. They don't like sunlight. They can't be in the sun all day. They need water. They can get **dehydrated**. This means they dry up. They get weak. Their hair falls out. Their skin flakes. They get sick. They die.

Mermaids don't like fire. They don't like bright lights. They don't like heat. They can't be burned when in water. But they can be burned on land.

So, they're rarely away from water. Water makes them strong. They like to stay safe. They like to be in control.

It's not uncommon for humans to give jewelry as gifts to mermaids.

A mermaid's weakest spot is the center of her head.

Mermaids are romantic. They love being in love. Since there aren't many mermen, they fall in love with humans. When in love, they lose their minds. They go to land. This makes them **vulnerable**. Vulnerable means weak. Some mermaids have lost their lives for love.

Mermaids are **vain**. Vain means they like how they look. They're easily tricked. They respond to **flattery**. Flattery is when people say good things. They love being called beautiful. Shiny things distract them.

SURVIVAL TIPS!

- Get to land. Mermaids are weakest on land.

- Don't travel across bodies of water. Avoid cruises or boat trips. Mermaids know how to get around in water. They have the advantage.

- Close your ears. Bring earplugs. Don't listen to them.

- Stay in your ship. Stay focused. Don't get distracted. One mistake could be deadly.

- Practice your swimming skills.

- Make sure you know exactly where you're going. Know how to use a compass. Know navigational skills. Don't get lost at sea.

- Get a mermaid to fall in love with a human male. They'll be distracted by love.

- Give mermaids sparkly gifts. This will keep them busy.

- Say many nice things. Compliment them.

Chapter Four

Mermaid Myths

What is the Aquatic Ape Theory? Who were the first mermaids? What are other stories about mermaid origins?

Nobody really knows how mermaids mate. Nobody knows how they're born.

A few people believe in the **Aquatic** Ape Theory. Aquatic means water. Some people connect this theory to mermaids. Humans came from apes. At first, these apes lived near water. Their bodies adapted for water life. They lost hair. They kept their heads above water. They developed fat under their skin. They developed large brains. This was from eating healthy seafood. They controlled their breathing like other sea animals. Most of these apes moved to land. They changed into humans. But some of these apes stayed in water. They changed into mermaids.

Dead mermaids have never been found. Their bodies rot quickly.

The first story about a fish-human was from the third century BCE. It was about Oannes. Oannes was a merman. He was a Babylonian god. He lived around the Persian Gulf. His human form was under his fish form. He left the sea during the day. He taught mankind wisdom. He went back to the sea at night.

The first mermaid was Atargartis. Her story came from ancient Syria. It started in 1000 BCE. Atargartis was a goddess. She fell in love with a human man. She accidentally killed him. She felt bad. She jumped into a lake. She wanted to become a fish. But the gods wouldn't let her give up her beauty. So, only her bottom half became a fish.

Pictures of Atargartis show her as a fishy human.

Know the Lingo!

- **Crustaceans:** animals that include crabs, lobsters, crayfish, shrimp, krill, and barnacles

- **Jezebel:** temptress

- **Kelpie:** water spirit in Scottish folk stories that looks like a horse and drowns travelers

- **Melusine:** French water spirit that was similar to a mermaid

- **Merrow:** Irish and English name for merfolk

- **Mollusks:** animals that include squids and octopuses

- **Naiad:** water nymph who lives in a river, spring, or waterfall

- **Nereid:** female spirit of seawater

- **Nymph:** female nature spirit

- **Nymphet:** an attractive young girl

- **Oceanid:** sea nymphs who were the daughters of giant Greek gods

- **Rusalka:** Russian word for mermaid

- **Selkies:** seals who could change into humans

- **Water elf:** another name for mermaid

Mermaid myths spread to other countries. Pacific Islanders believed humans came from merfolk. Merfolk lost their tails. They magically walked on land.

Irish people believed St. Patrick created mermaids. St. Patrick helped bring Christianity to Ireland. Some women didn't believe in Christianity. St. Patrick turned them into mermaids.

In a Native American myth, two girls disobeyed their mother. They went swimming. They were punished. They were turned into mermaids. They had to tow their parents' canoe.

There are many different ideas about how mermaids came to be.

Chapter Five

Fishy Tales

Who is Hans Christian Andersen?

Hans Christian Andersen wrote fairy tales. He wrote *The Little Mermaid*. This is a famous mermaid story.

Andersen's mermaid saved a drowning prince. She fell in love with him. She went to a sea witch. She wanted legs. She traded her voice. Her tongue was cut out. The prince chose another woman. The mermaid was fated to die from a broken heart. She was given a chance to save herself. Her sisters went to the sea witch. They traded their hair for a magical knife. The mermaid had to stab the prince. She had to bathe in his blood. She couldn't do it. She died. She became sea foam.

Walking on land was like walking on knives for the little mermaid.

Real-World Connection

Weeki Wachee Springs is in South Florida. It's a family fun park. It has a special pool of water. Mermaids swim in the pool! These women are professional mermaids. Their job is to pretend to be mermaids. They swim using air hoses. These air hoses help them breathe underwater. They perform every day. They wear 6-foot-long (1.8 meters) mermaid tails. They do synchronized swimming acts. This means they swim together. They make the same swimming moves. They do spinning moves. They do a lot of tricks. They even eat and drink underwater. The Weeki Wachee mermaids have been swimming for over 60 years. The first show was in 1947. In the beginning, the mermaids went to the street. They lured travelers to come see the show. Then, they jumped into the water. Their motto is: Once a mermaid, always a mermaid.

Today's stories about mermaids are **sightings**. People say they've seen mermaids. They share their reports. Even Christopher Columbus thought he saw mermaids.

In 1967, boat passengers saw a mermaid. They were in British Columbia. They said the mermaid was eating salmon. They said it had a porpoise's tail.

In 2009, several people saw a mermaid. They were near Israel. They saw it leaping. They saw it doing tricks in the air. A nearby town offered a $1 million award for proof.

Mermaids are mysterious. Don't fall under their spells!

People want to believe in mermaids.

Did You Know?

- The color of a mermaid's tail reflects her mood.

- Aquamarines are gemstones. Some people think these gemstones are mermaids' tears. They used aquamarines as lucky charms on sea trips.

- Some people believe in maidmers. Maidmers are creatures. They have the top half of a fish. They have the bottom half of a woman. They're the opposite of mermaids.

- Some people want to swim like a mermaid. There are schools that teach how.

- There's a Little Mermaid statue in Denmark. It celebrates Hans Christian Andersen. It's a popular tourist attraction.

- Coney Island is in New York. It hosts a Mermaid Parade. The parade started in 1983. It celebrates the beginning of summer. Each year, there's a king merman and a queen mermaid.

- In 2012, the U.S. National Ocean Service stated there's no evidence of mermaids.

- Blackbeard was a pirate. Some people think he ordered his ships to avoid mermaids.

- Warsaw is a city in Poland. It has a mermaid on its official city seal.

Consider This!

Take a Position: Read the 45th Parallel Press book about fairies. Some people believe that mermaids are a special type of fairy. They think mermaids are water fairies. Do you agree or disagree? Argue your point with reasons and evidence.

Say What? Explain how mermaids are like fish. Explain how they're like humans. Do you think they're more humans or fish? Explain your reasoning.

Think About It! In some stories, mermaids are peaceful and beautiful. In other stories, mermaids are evil. Do you think they're more good or evil? What do mermaids reveal about human nature?

Learn More

* Berk, Ari. *The Secret History of Mermaids and Creatures of the Deep*. Somerville, MA: Candlewick Press, 2009.

* Osbourne, Mary Pope, and Troy Howell (illustrator). *Mermaid Tales from Around the World*. New York: Scholastic, 1999.

* Virtue, Doreen. *Mermaids 101: Exploring the Magical Underwater World of the Merpeople*. Carlsbad, CA: Hay House, 2012.

Glossary

ageless (AYJ-lis) never growing old

aquatic (uh-KWAT-ik) related to water

dehydrated (dee-HYE-dray-tid) losing water, drying up

flattery (FLAT-ur-ee) complimenting for gain

hypnotize (HIP-nuh-tize) to put others in a trance in order to control them

immortal (ih-MOR-tuhl) able to live forever

merfolk (MUR-foke) mermaids and mermen

mermen (MUR-men) male versions of mermaids

shapeshifters (SHAYP-shift-urz) creatures that can change their shapes

shimmer (SHIM-ur) to shine, to glitter

sightings (SITE-ingz) reports of having seen something

Siren (SYE-ruhn) half-woman and half-bird creature from Greek myths that lured sailors to their deaths; another word for vamp

tridents (TRY-dents) three-pronged spears

vain (VAYN) liking how one looks too much

vamp (VAMP) temptress, a woman who seduces men for gain

vulnerable (VUHL-nur-uh-buhl) weak

Index

About the Author

Dr. Virginia Loh-Hagan is an author, university professor, former classroom teacher, and curriculum designer. Her favorite fairy tale is "The Little Mermaid." She lives in San Diego with her very tall husband and very naughty dogs. To learn more about her, visit www.virginialoh.com.